MAZE

FOR KIDS

MAZE BOOK

Milk

MILK

Milk

Milk

MILK

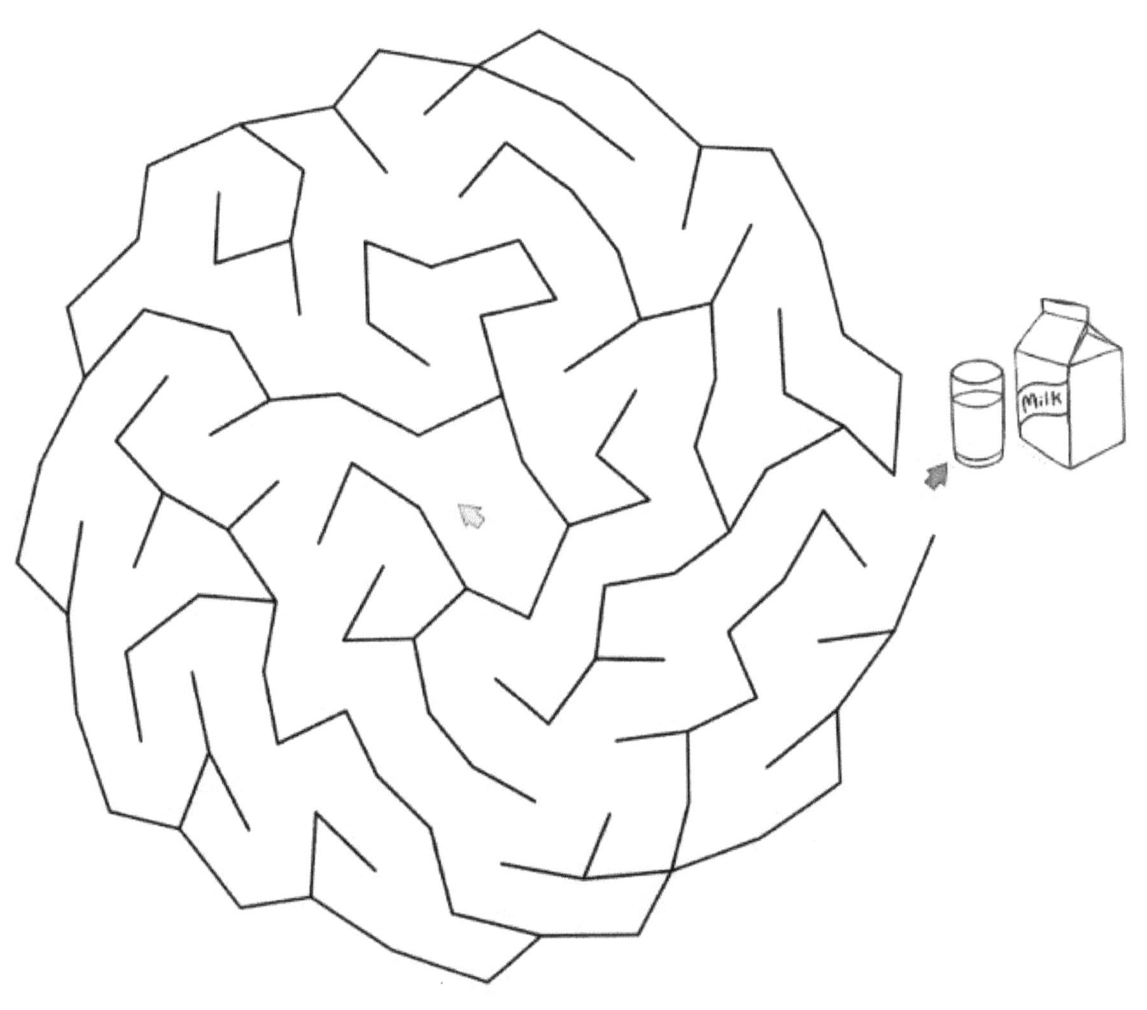

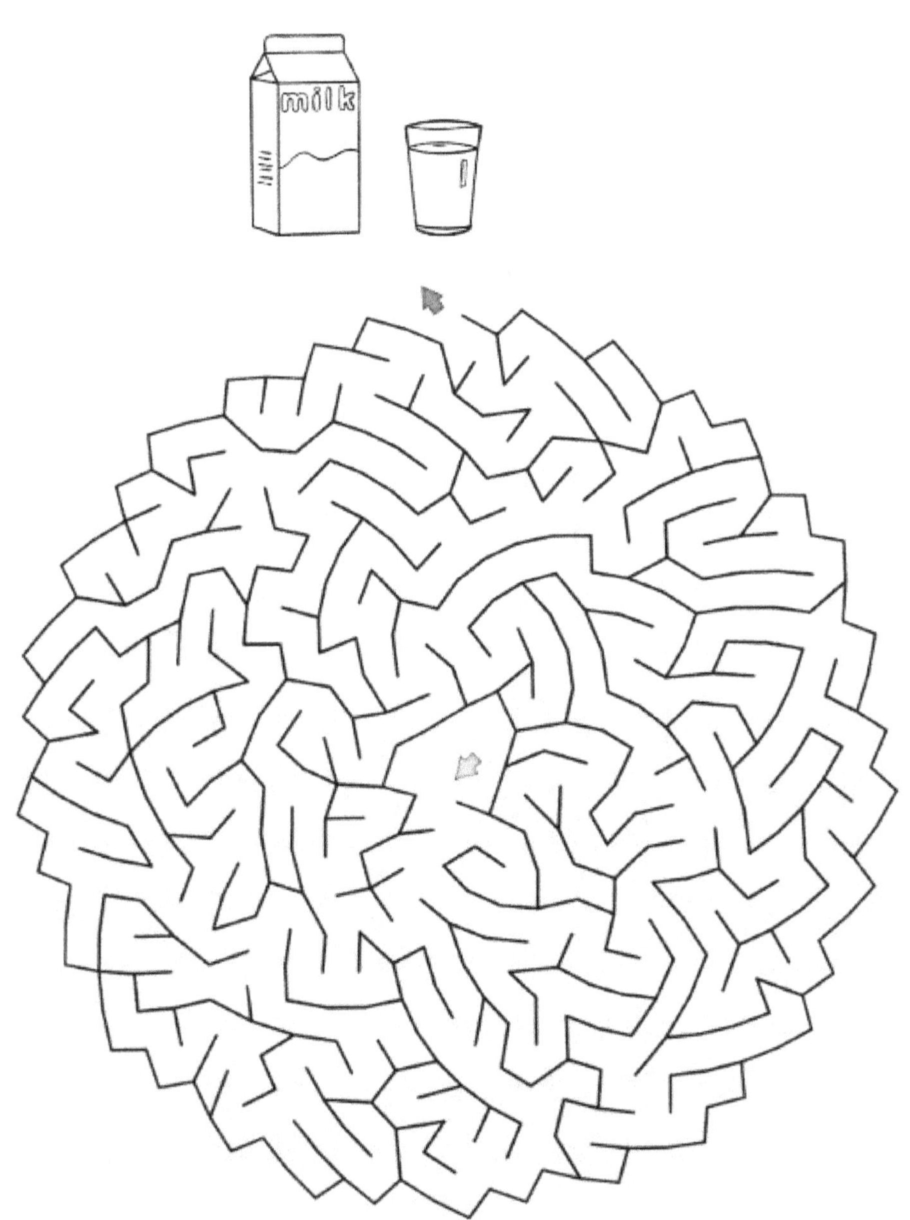

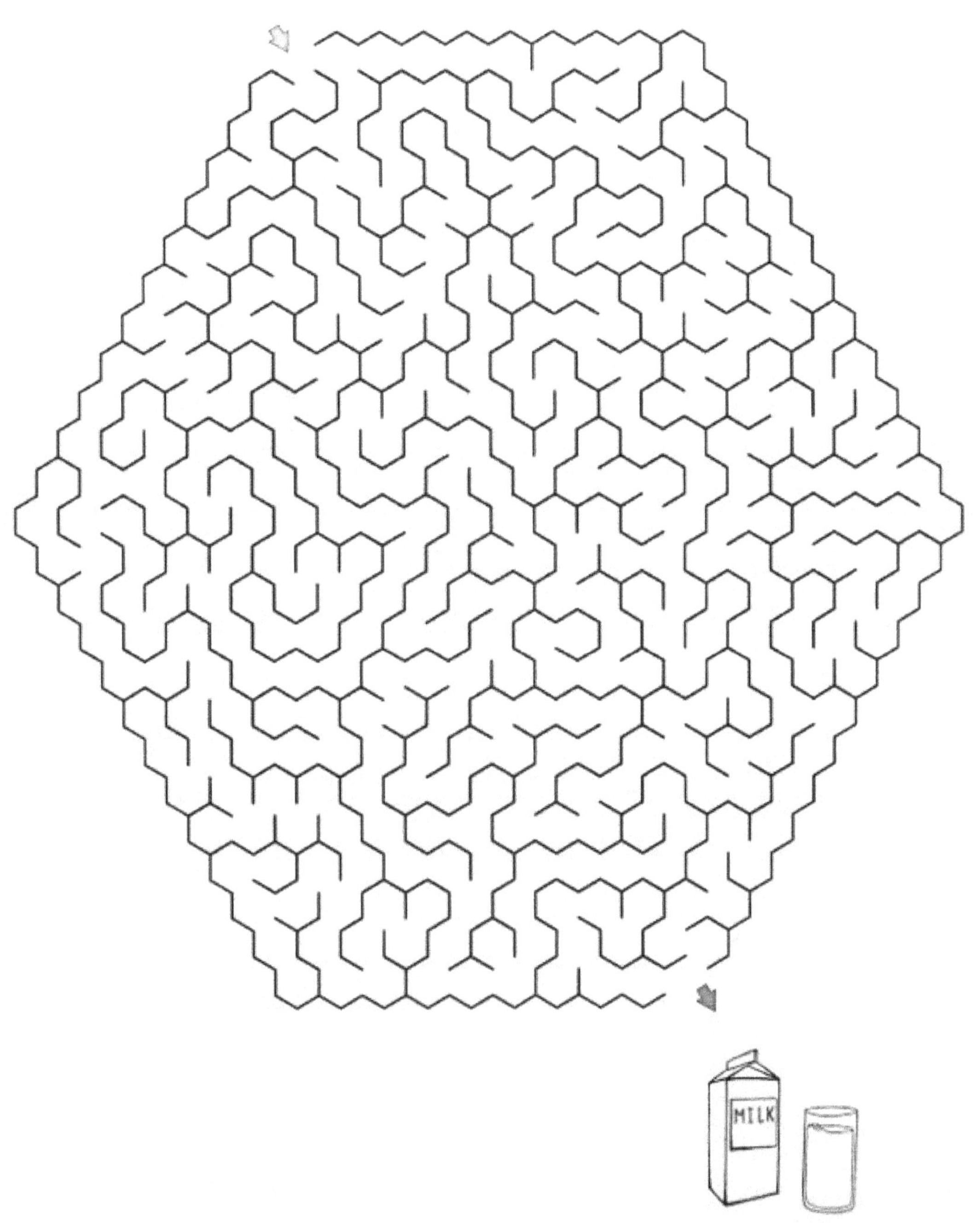

Milk

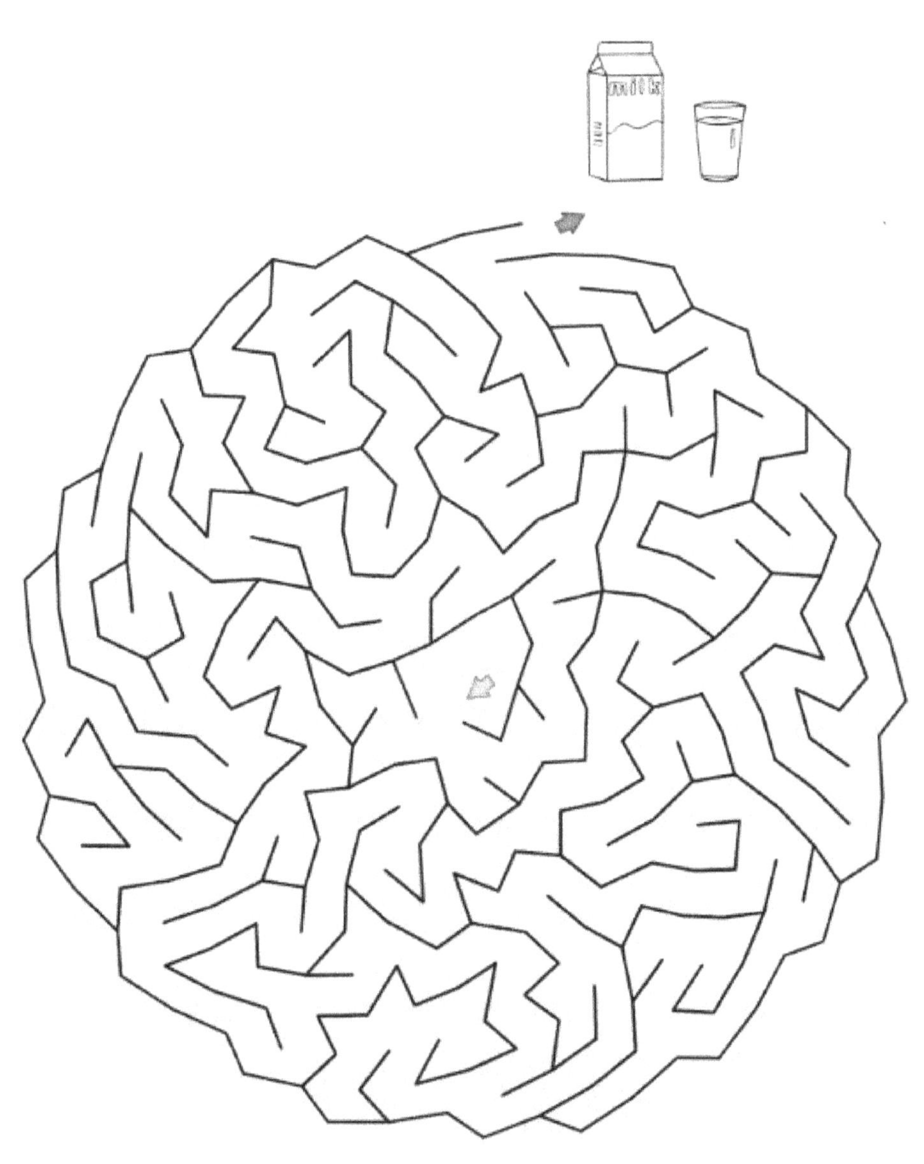

Milk

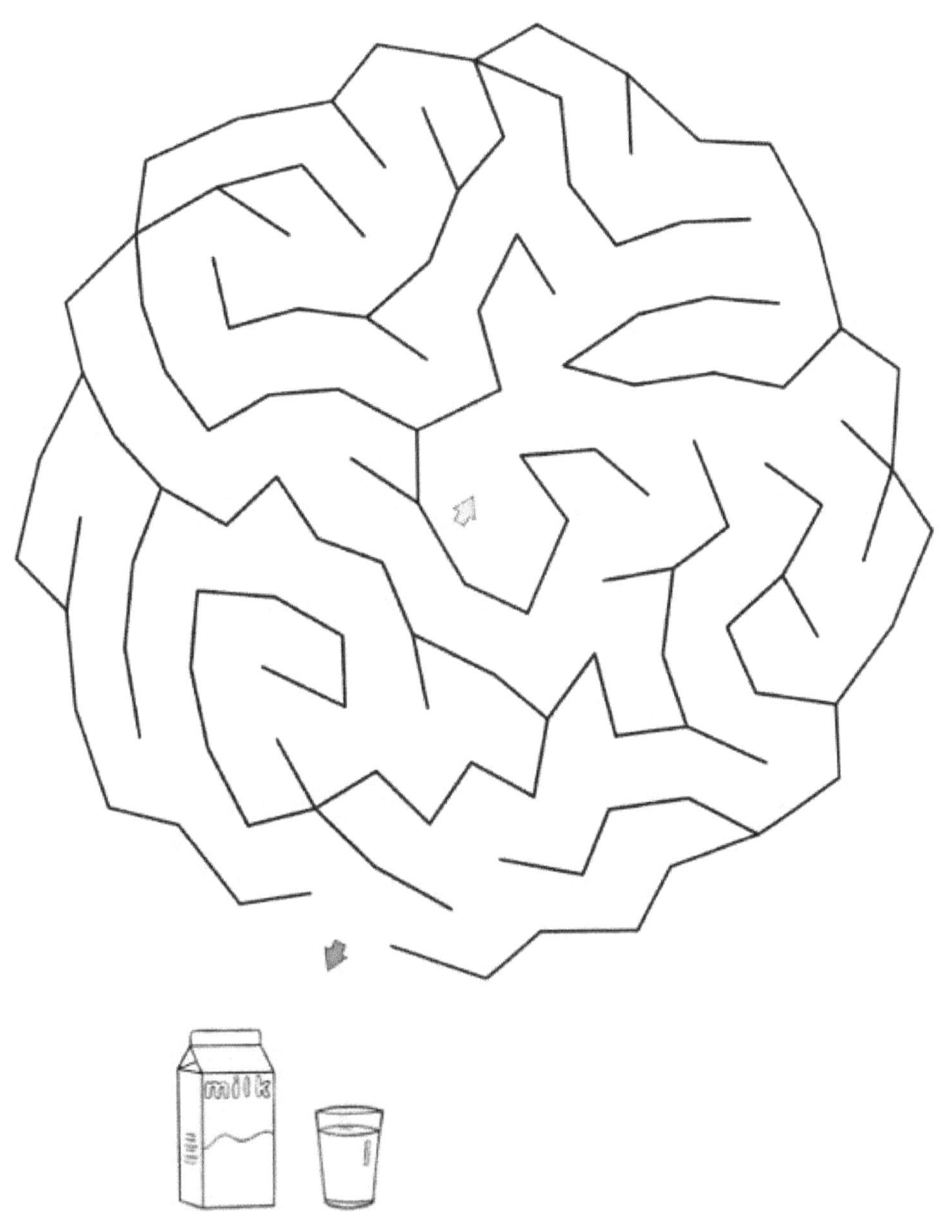

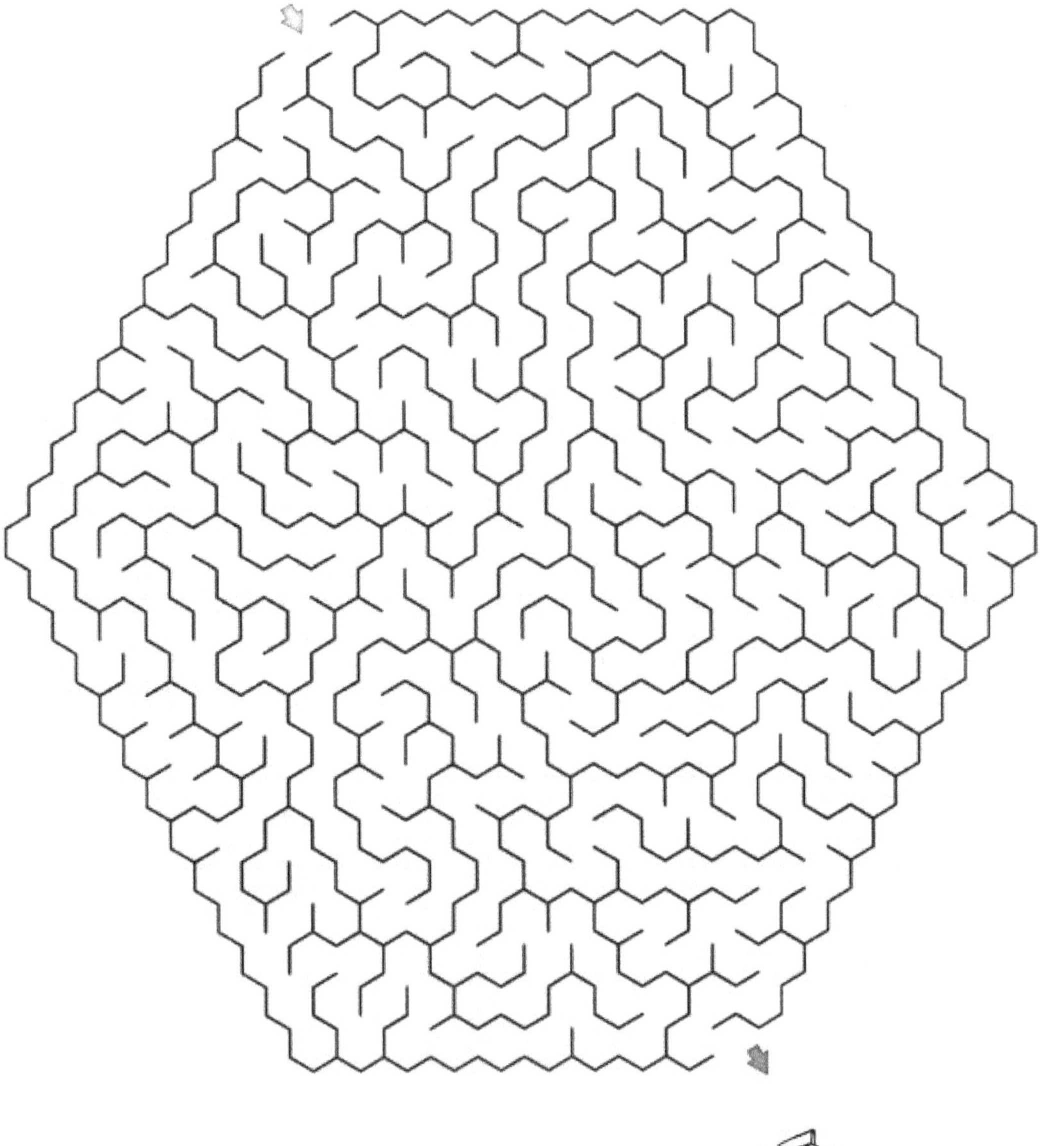

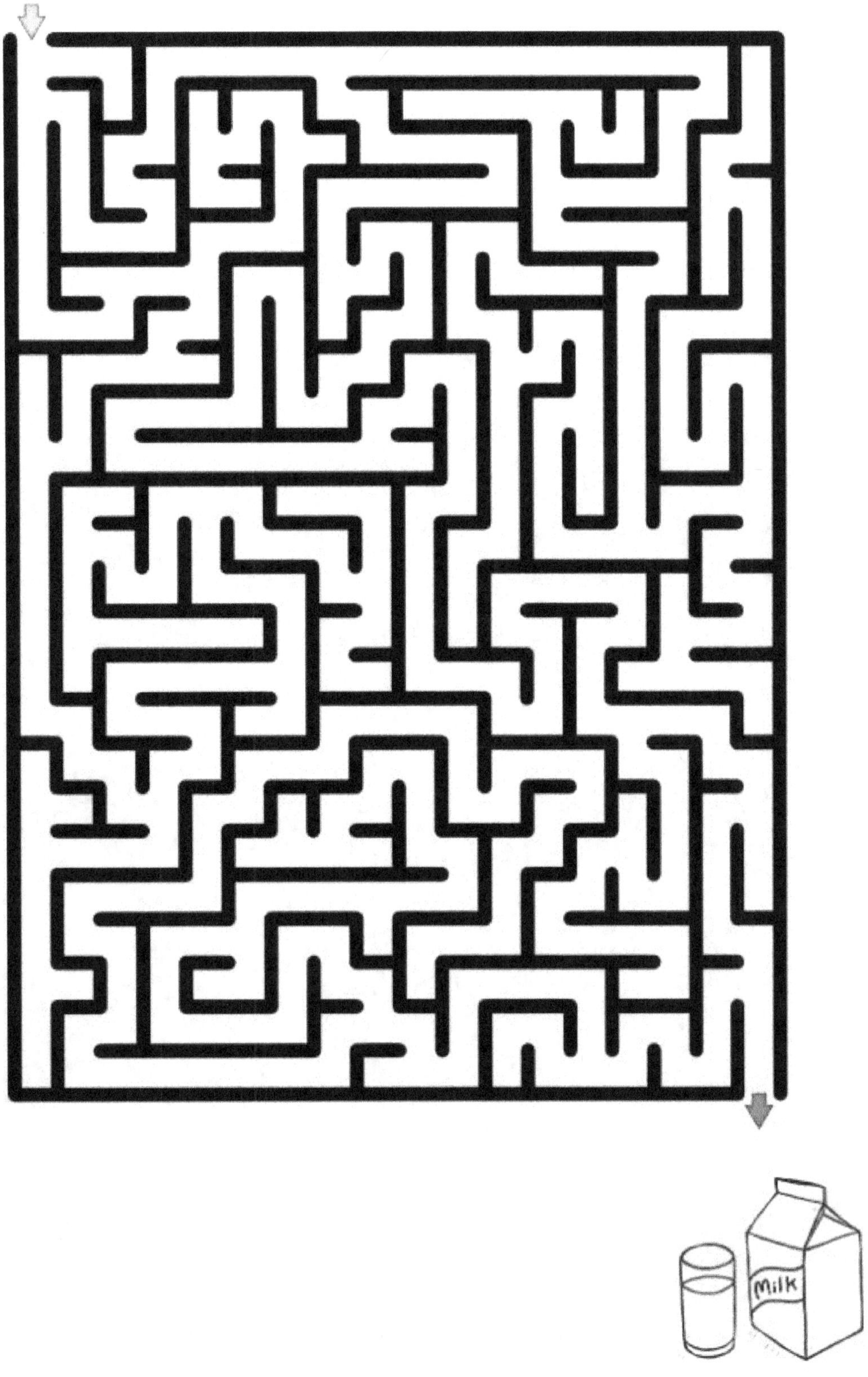

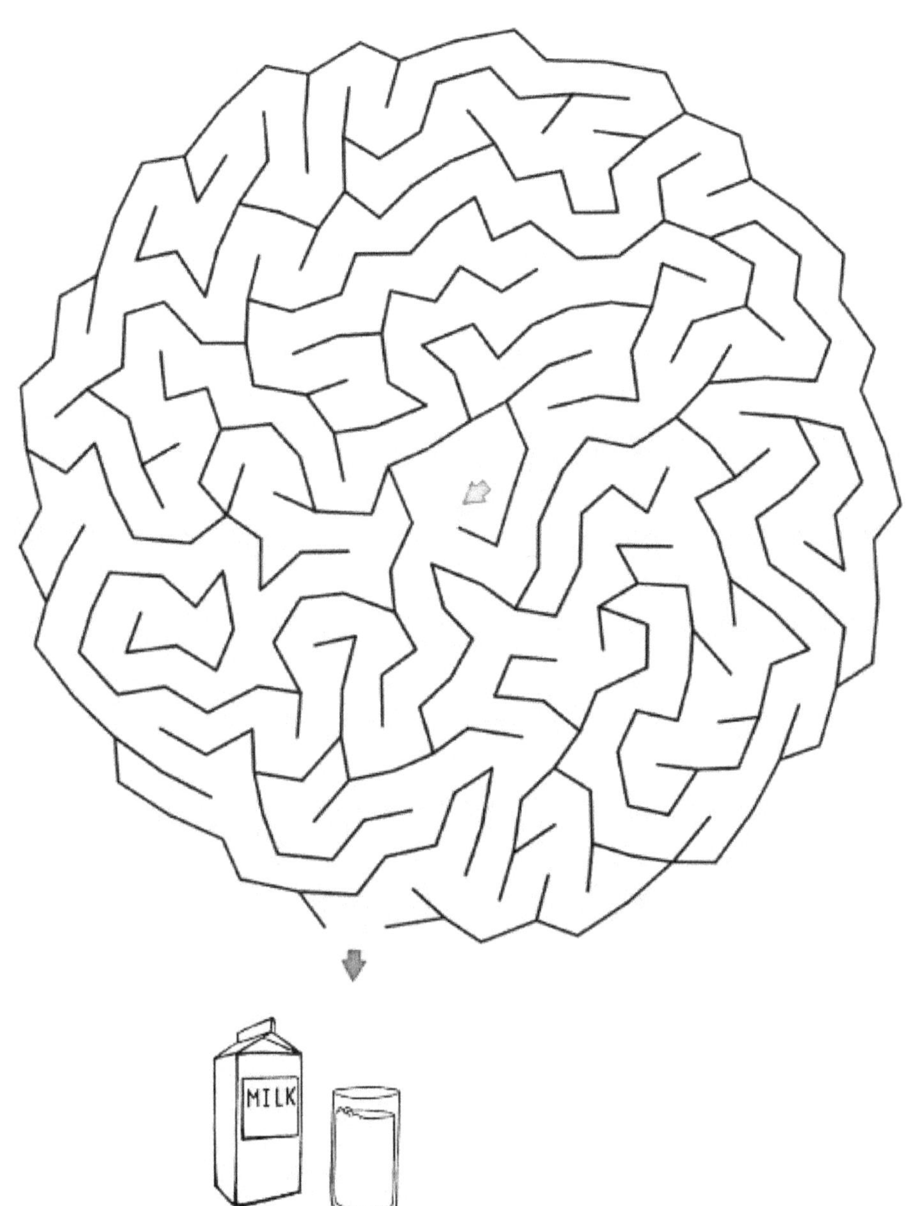

MILK

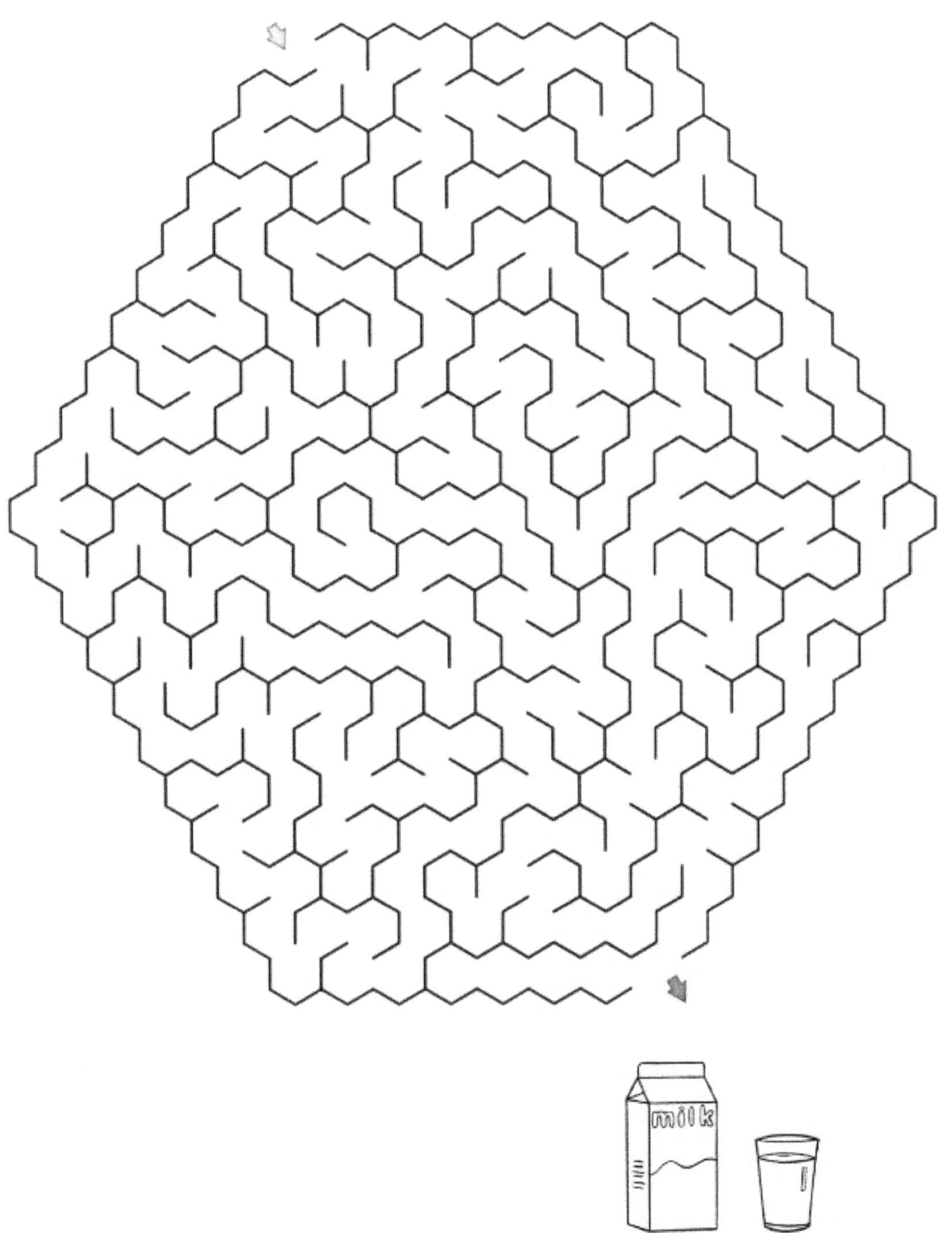

Milk

MILK

milk

milk

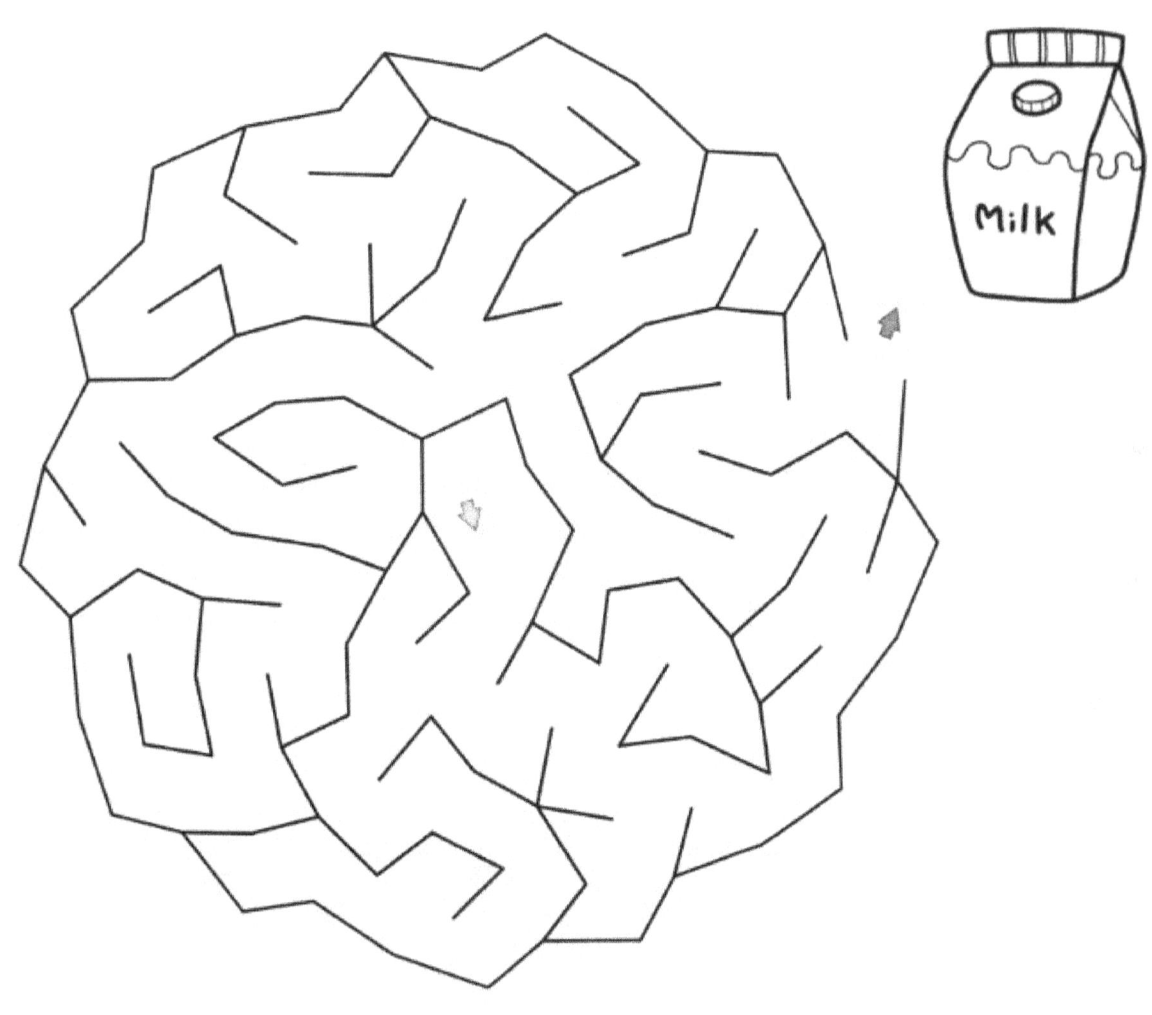

Milk